Making balloon animals at my brother's Cub Scouts (Pack 320) movie night.

Making balloon animals at Sunrise Little League.

Hi, I'm Isabella! I'm an 11 year old Girl Scout Junior in Troop 3216. I made this project for my **Bronze Award**. It's the highest award a Junior can earn and it takes a long time to do: 20 hours minimum of work!

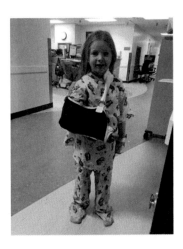

For my Bronze Award, I decided to look over things that happened to me and combine them with stuff that I'm passionate about. I love making balloon animals, and because I ended up with a hospital stay when I was 6 years old at Children's Hospital Los Angeles (CHLA), I decided to write a book teaching kids in hospitals how to make balloon animals. I held fundraising events where I made balloon animals on the spot to fund this book so that I could donate copies to CHLA!

I hope you enjoy learning how to make balloon animals, and I was glad to share my experience with you :)

Sincerely,

Isabella Warth

D1737705

1 **Stretch** the balloon in front of your body **several times**, as wide as possible.

This step is **VERY** important! If you don't do it, the balloon could **pop** in your face!

2 Put the pump between your legs to **keep it steady**.

3 Now, carefully **stretch** the neck of the balloon over the nozzle of the pump.

4 With one hand, hold the **neck** of the balloon tightly to the pump...

... use the other hand to grip the **base** of the pump.

Now it's time to **inflate** your balloon.

5 While keeping a firm grip with both hands...

... raise and lower your top hand over and over again.

6 Stop when you have about 2" of **uninflated** "tail" left.

7 Carefully remove the balloon off of the pump,

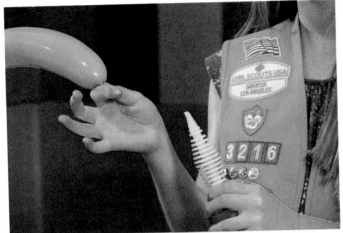

Easy peasy!

Make sure you keep a **tight grip** on the neck of the balloon!

Now it's time to **tie the knot!** If this part is too tricky, ask a grownup for help.

8 Let a bit of air out (you will hear a **shrieking sound)** to give yourself more length to tie with.

9 Wrap the neck of the balloon in a complete circle around **two fingers**.

10 Now take the very end of the neck...

... and push it through the middle of your two fingers to make the knot.

Now you have a **tied balloon**!

TA-DA!

Here comes the fun part —

making your **balloon animal**!

11 Tug on both ends of the inflated balloon to **straighten** it out.

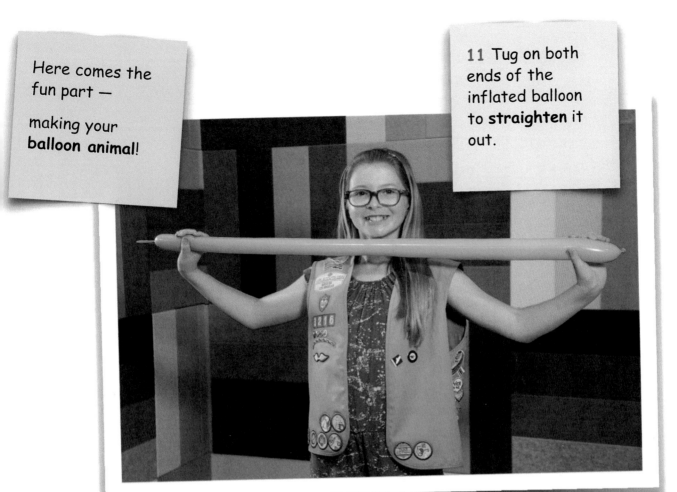

Time for your 1st twist! Don't worry if it comes undone, you'll have an **indent line** to try again!

First twist, check ✔

12 With your right hand placed about 3" from the tied end of the balloon...

... use your left hand to **twist** the small end of the balloon 5 times.

13 Hold the balloon 5" from your 1st twist and **bend** this section in half.

14 Keeping the balloon bent in your hand, **extend** your grip to grab the 1st twist back into the same hand.

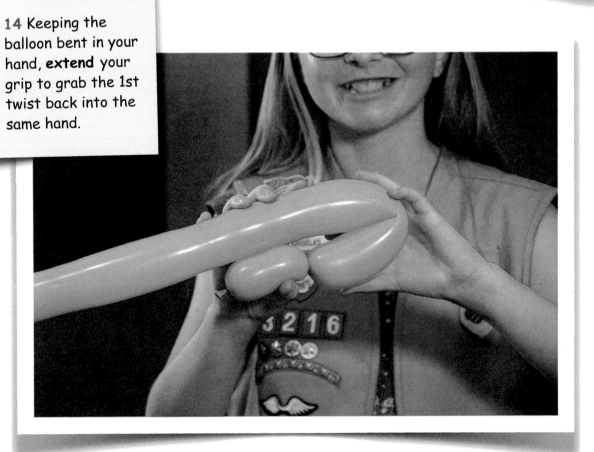

15 While holding all of these pieces together, **double twist** everything together **5 times.**

You've made ears!

Time to make the neck!

16 With your **right hand**, hold the balloon 1" down from the head to make your next twist.

... then grab the 1" section with your **left hand** and **twist** the balloon **5 times**.

Here's a **trick** I like to use to make life **easier** for the next step.

Hold the neck of the dog between your knees so you have your **hands free** for the next twist.

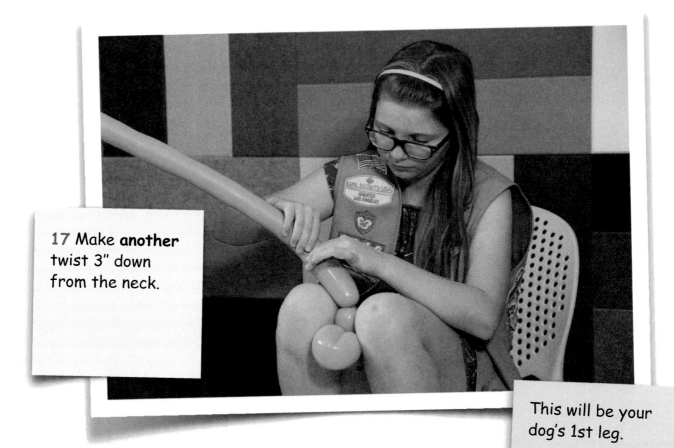

17 Make **another** twist 3" down from the neck.

This will be your dog's 1st leg.

18 Make **another** twist 1" down.

(This will be your dog's 1st foot.)

19 Make **one more** twist 1" down.

(This will be your dog's 2nd foot).

20 Now **fold** the entire balloon so both feet are pointing **upwards**.

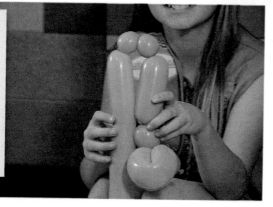

Now it's time for another **double twist**!

21 Grab all of the animal where the neck meets the 1st leg...

... hold onto the long part and make a **double twist** to finish the 2nd leg.

Looking good!

Now it's time to make the **body**

22 Make another twist 3" down — as in the previous step, **twist it twice** here to secure it.

Now let's make the **back legs**.

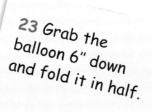

23 Grab the balloon 6" down and fold it in half.

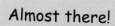
Almost there!

24 Grip everything at the end of the body and **twist 3** times.

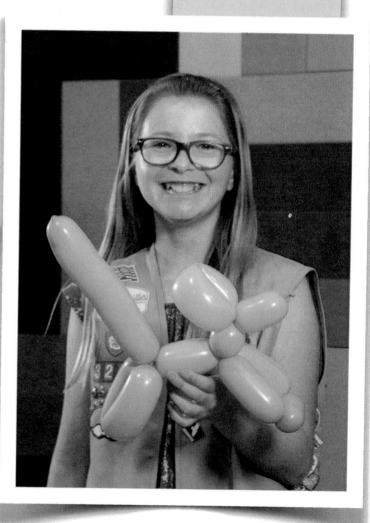

25 To make the **tail** look cute, you can curve it back towards the body.

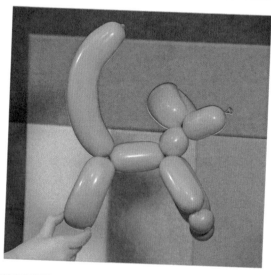

TA-DAAA!!

Now you have your very own **balloon dog**!

26 For added fun, draw a face on your balloon dog with a **sharpie**.

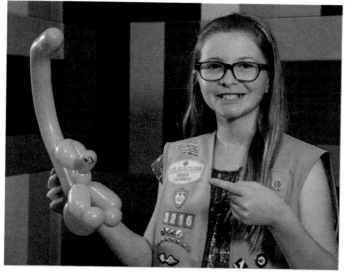

And that's it!
Congratulations on making your first balloon animal!!!

Ready for more? I have created a **YouTube** channel where you can learn how to make all kinds of balloon animals.

Here's a link:

... and here's the dog you just made:

Maybe you're in the mood for a **stylish hat?**

Ahoy, matey!

Time to fight off some pirates with our **balloon swords**!

... and a **palm tree** that he can climb!

Let's make a **monkey** ...

Made in the USA
Las Vegas, NV
14 September 2023

77544053R10017